I am Hmong Copyright © 2024 by Kha Yang Xiong

All rights reserved. No part of this book may be reproduced or used in any manner without written permission from the copyright owner.

First printing edition Feb 2024

Hardcover Book ISBN: 978-1-7342450-8-0
Softcover Book   ISBN: 978-1-7342450-9-7

Design and illustrations by Lue Vang
Published by Hmong Children's Books

www.hmongchildrensbook.com

Dedication

To all the children in the world, may you forever cherish your heritage, culture, and language, embracing them with pride and keeping them dear to your heart.
K.Y.X.

To community, family and friends loving us into being.
xLus

KUV NOJ MOV.
I EAT RICE.

About the Author

Dr. Kha Yang Xiong was born in a Hmong village in the hills of Laos. At the end of the Vietnam War, her family fled to escape persecution and settled in the refugee camps of Thailand. When she was seven years old, her family immigrated to the United States. Currently, Kha is supporting educators in language instruction to English learners and multilingual children. She received her doctorate degree from the University of Colorado Denver with a focus on equity in education. She is passionate about helping children learn about their heritage, culture, and language. Kha is on a journey to make books to teach about the Hmong people.

About the Artist

Lu/xLus was born in Ban Vinai Refugee Camp and grew up in Clovis, CA. He trained in photography and multimedia at Defense Information School, and served in the US Marine Corps at Quantico's Combat Visual Information Center. His career spans education, non-profit, tech and startups. He is Co-Founder of Hmongstory Legacy and artist collective Kilo Company. He directed feature films The Hmong and the Secret War and Yia The Bull Mua. His collection of short stories, comics, music, and art in *Tigers From The Mountain* is inspired by Hmong folklore, diaspora, community and family.

www.hmongchildrensbook.com

www.ingramcontent.com/pod-product-compliance
Lightning Source LLC
LaVergne TN
LVRC090147080526
838200LV00093B/367